AF111122

PEOPLE FINDER, BUFFALO

PEO

PEOPLE FINDER, BUFFALO

FIND

BUF

PLE

ISBN: 979-8-218-39199-7
CLOAK.WTF

ER,

JOE HALL

ALO

❶ **Shimoda, Brandon. "Curse for the Guard." The Asian American Literary Review, Spring/Summer 2018, pp. 14**

These poems come to you from the provincial city of Buffalo. Buffalo's municipal information infrastructure has largely collapsed. People here have few ways of knowing about their city, which means we live in increasingly different cities. Multiplicity can be beautiful, but delusion is not. Dwelling in different cities a few feet apart makes it hard to get together, hard to mobilize, hard to change anything at all. In this way Buffalo is not much different than many other small and mid-sized cities. So these poems aim to keep stories about Buffalo in circulation. And when I say stories, I mean dirt. These poems garbage the most garbage people and organizations in Buffalo.

To do so, the text names names. I settled on this strategy after reading Brandon Shimoda's essay "Curse for the Guard," specifically, this sentence: "The murderers (both individuals and the systems to which they were reporting) reaped the benefit of passing into oblivion."[1] Implicit in Shimoda's essay is the fact that power structures legitimize or, at the very least, shelter the violences done by them and their members. It suggests what those whose violence is officially sanctioned desire is the benefit of oblivion. The benefit of oblivion. Naming them, naming what they did, and, for Shimoda, tying, forever, the murderer to their victim, is a curse. However, departing from Shimoda, these poems replace the victim with the victimizer. You can see my spasmodic settler brain at work, given how my imagination fails to do anything but dwell on what these people have done by imagining them doing it onto themselves. Fuck, with all due diligence, these fuckers.

You may not know the names in the poem, so feel welcome to fill in the names of members of your own city and/or county power structure in this order: racist developer, white supremacist Sheriff, crime panic business association, corrupt machine politician, killer cops, and—can we name the biggest thing of all, can it be held by any name?—racial capitalism in the imperial core. Tell me what I get wrong.

Yrs,
Joe

THE BUFFALO RENAISSANCE[i]

can't dream the economy because is good they might repo the economy your bed
is good can't dream because the economy is they might repo your good dreams they economy is
can't dream because you good the had the bad to get a second economy
to make rent the

that the body dream can be free—where all economies somebody
are free—the common, common
in that freedom, economy communion only dream in that
repo freedom in that freedom repo could only be—

[i] The term "Buffalo Renaissance" is a marketing tactics employed by local business and government. Renaissance refers to the opportunities available to members of Buffalo's ruling class in reorganizing the city's economy around hospitals, universities, jacking up the rent, and the city's relentless transfer of public wealth to private hands. Above all, there is no plan to make life better for the majority of Buffalonians; there's only what David Harvey calls the disposal of surplus capital into "a mindless form of urbanization"—relentless demolition and building that maintains the current relations of production and increases inequality (i.e. an opportunity to jack up rents/the rate of profit). Through this Renaissance, the city has remained staggeringly poor, moving from the 2nd to 3rd poorest city in the nation not because of its increasing wealth but because its neighbor along Lake Erie, Cleveland, grew poorer.

CARL PALADINO, DEVELOPER, DISGRACED EX-BUFFALO SCHOOLBOARD MEMBER[i]

Carl P, Ki Ki, hangs at J.T's fungus
mouth, J.T.'s normy horror
value cube urban slash J.T.'s Carl Paladino hangs out at
the dismal horizon of stage 4 Italian gentroids.
You can. You can. 905 Elmwood. barfight.

[i] Each provincial city in this empire has its own wretched ruling set. Paladino is one such creature, having built his wealth on land deals, construction, landlordism and slumlordism. He translates this wealth into reactionary political projects. He routinely bankrolls national and local far right candidates. In 2013, he joined the school board of the Buffalo Public Schools to steer it toward school privatization projects, from which he profited. Paladino also maintains informal ties with the local fascist organization the New York Watchmen.

TIM HOWARD, EX-SHERIFF OF ERIE COUNTY, NY; WALES, NY TOWN SUPERVISOR[i]

Tim Howard arrests Tim Howard for murder
and spends the night looking the other other way
as Tim Howard knocks Tim Howard's head against
the hardness of the Erie County holding center
whispering, *murderer, murderer, murderer.*

[i] From 2005 to the end of 2021, thirty-four people died in the Erie County Holding Center under Sheriff Tim Howard. Many died under suspicious circumstances (i.e. guards murdered them or orchestrated their medical neglect, including denying life-sustaining medications or ignoring statements that they wanted to kill themselves): Nathan Frailey (53), Daniel McNeil (age unknown), Marlon Clay (35), Michael G. Roberts (49), Joseph Balbuzoski (37), Robert J. Henchen (42), Joann L. Jesse (48), John Reardon (53), Marguerite "Margie" Arrindell (54), Adam Murr (31), Daniel Nye (26), Jeremy Kiekbush (29), Keith John (26), Rakim Scriven (18), Trevell Walker (36), Lester J. Foster (47), Kristian "Mookie" "Slater" Woods (40), Edward Berezowski (54), Patrick Yale (49), Richard A. Metcalf Jr. (35), RosieLee Yvette Mendez (26), David Liddick (42), India Cummings (27), Vincent Sorrentino (31), David Stitt (63), Michael J. Girard (33), Joseph E. Bialaszewski (29), Connell Burrell (44), Daniel Spicola (40), Robert Ingalsbe (33), Michael "Mikey" Frears (27), James Ellis (58).

THE ALLENTOWN ARTS FESTIVAL[i]

The Allentown Arts Festival finds Allentown too queer, trans, butch,
and nonbinary and lodges a zoning complaint to evict
Allentown from Allentown so Allentown can quietly
be plaque in a dead, appropriately affluent organ.

[i] In 2017 the going explanation for what would result in the closure of Dreamland, an LGBTQ+ art space in a historical LGBTQ+ neighborhood in Buffalo, was a complaint from the Allentown Arts Festival.

PIGS[1]

Officer Tedesco stops Officer McAlister outside of
his house in Kenmore, his house from
which an American flag flies with one blue bar.
Officer Tedesco demands Officer McAlister
stop and show him his hands.
Officer Tedesco then beats Officer McAlister within
an inch of his life so Officer Parisi, who
was circling Mang Park, steps out
of his vehicle and shoots
Officer Tedesco 38 times.
Officers Parisi & McAlister write a false report at the station.
Officer Tedesco files a false report in hell.
Narcotics detective Joseph Cook, during a drunk
no-knock raid on the police station, stumbles and kills officers
Parisi & Tedesco. They are all thrown
a parade by the Minister of Flies.
All the people come to lick their shining leather
while the chief of police reads collaborative fiction.
Applause.

[1] Pigs do what pigs do in big cities and here, in the provinces. In 2018, Buffalo Police Officer Justin Tedesco (salary: 101k) open fired on and killed Jose Hernandez-Rossy as he fled. Hernandez-Rossy was unarmed. In 2017, Officers McAlister (salary: 138k) and Parisi (salary: 112k) killed Wardel Davis after an unwarranted stop. Narcotics detective Joseph Cook (salary: 128k) "was single-handedly responsible for more dog deaths than all the reported incidents in the New York City in 2011-2012 alone." Over one three year stretch, Cook shot and killed 25 dogs. And here in the provinces, as in big cities, police violence is rewarded, excused, or swept under the rug. City spending on police rose 54% between 2006 and 2020. In 2021 the mayoral administration proposed a modest haircut to BPD in the wake of the 2020 uprisings then promptly walked these cuts back in 2022 by proposing a $90.7 million funding increase for the BPD.

ULYSSES S. WINGO, FORMER BUFFALO COMMON COUNCIL MEMBER[i]

Ulysses S. Wingo got spotted by ShotSpotter
spying on Ulysses S. Wingo as Ulysses S.
Wingo slobbered on the wingtips of the mayor slobbering on the
wingtips of anyone w/a fat stack of cash & a wrecking
ball as the cops arrive that ShotSpotter called
catching it all in its auditory radius, which
demands the killing of trees to unimpede
its hallucinations of danger—you go to say
this to Ulysses S. Wingo but he's gone,
he was never there, emptied out
into a suit that carried money's silver echo
that calls to the eye that calls to the gun
that makes sure the money goes where the money
always goes—up next to fill the suit a new
name that always becomes Ulysses S. Wingo
in the Council Chamber Hall: 65
Niagara Sq.

[i] Buffalo's electeds responded to calls to defund the police by doing the opposite. In 2022 Buffalo Common Council Member Ulysses S. Wingo doubled down on his commitment to a pilot program to utilize ShotSpotter in his majority Black Masten district, even after the Common Council pulled funding for the program after withering public criticism. The Shotspotter system involves installing an array of microphones throughout public spaces for the ostensible purpose of detecting gunshots. Numerous reports have found the technology does not work: it's a false alarm machine. What it does do is increase surveillance of Black and Latinx communities, increase police activity via its false alarms, and increase the chances of police inflicting violence on these communities. Shortly after his unpopular ShotSpotter campaign, Wingo announced he wouldn't be running for re-election.

BYRON BROWN, MAYOR OF BUFFALO (2005-PRESENT)[i]

Mayor Byron Browns tiptoes to either side of an office door
listening to their listening, their ears' whorls
mirrored in intense circulations of silence—one
Byron Brown knocks, the other gasps,
tiptoes away from the door, hides
under his desk and to keep calm practices
his signature with his finger. The other Byron Brown
wanders the chambers of City Hall
with the words of every city resident
folded into the blossoms of his pocket:
longer bus routes, better service, lower rent,
no checkpoints, no lying, killer cops.
Other Byron Brown, under his desk,
sketches the final details of the celebration
of the massive transfer of wealth from the people of Buffalo
to some shitheel builder. Byron Brown rolls the plans
into two small cylinders, sticks them in his ears, and says,
"Byron Brown," in the twilight of under his desk.
Soon enough, there they are, in the paper:
Byron Brown, rich people, and a building.

[i] In almost twenty years under Brown's administration, the poverty rate in the city has not budged; in 2020, the childhood poverty rate was 43.4%. According to *Investigative Post*, over the course of fifteen years from 2005 to 2020, "the city's spending on police has effectively defunded other city services."

THOMAS FEELEY, WESTERN NEW YORK ICE FIELD DIRECTOR UNTIL 2021 [i]

COVID rages in Buffalo Federal Detention and Thomas Feeley doesn't order soap, doesn't
have masks, Thomas Feeley says he has masks, that he has made it rain
soap, Thomas Feeley sits in a cell sick as shit,
the solution to himself, Thomas Feeley says, is not freedom, not those
who could hold you with care but a cell in solitary, half a doctor
and turning away the health department so the prison house of himself
can hold the virus, Thomas Feeley crams
Thomas Feeley into a bus not bound for care but another jail
across the country, trucking COVID, Thomas Feeley
finally gives way, kicks himself out of a van, at the Citgo
by the I-90, free and cashless, the Greyhound gone
Thomas Feeley, has not given himself
a mask and Citgo won't let Thomas Feeley hang out
inside, Thomas Feeley mills around
the pumps, asks strangers
for cash, for a ticket, their eyes tighten
over crinkled masks, Thomas Feeley has left Thomas Feeley
hungry and in the dark, this is the only condition
in which Thomas Feeley lets Thomas Feeley be free.

[i] The revolutionary George Jackson's Blood In My Eye forwards two startling formulations. The first is that the United States is the world's most developed fascist nation and that we don't see this because its totalitarian rule is only occasionally contested. That contestation, when it exudes a whiff of revolutionary ardor, is always met with overwhelming force: "Facism has established itself in a most disguised and efficient manner in this country. It feels so secure that the leaders allow us the luxury of a faint protest. Take protest too far, however, and they will show their other face. Doors will be kicked down in the night and machine gun fire and buckshot will become the medium of exchange." Take the backlash to the uprisings in Ferguson and in 2020 including the likely assassination of Ferguson activists, relentlessly expanding police budgets, Cop City in Atlanta, more Cop Cities on the way, RICO charges for activists "writing zines" and practicing "collectivism," the assassination of Forest Defender Tortuguita, and the relentless supply of arms for Israel to use in its genocide of Palestinians and criminalization of protests against genocide at home. Jackson's other formulation, a companion

to Ruth Wilson Gilmore's expansive definition of the prison industrial complex, is the term "the pig class." The pig class? The reactionary right within the working class: "The top-heavy bureaucratic agencies that exist with quasi social sanction—and in particular the ones that are given over to the maintenance of law and order—draw their principal personnel from the pig class and consequently are an expression of that class's mentality: a stagnant, even atavistic mentality that is completely dependent upon regimen and rote to perform the simplest of functions. First of all, the opposition is stupid. However, let me qualify that statement with the observation that they make up for what they lack in brains with sheer brutality." Thomas Feeley, an ICE bureaucrat, is an excellent example of the brutality of the pig class. This poem chronicles the many actions Feeley took to try to wound the lives of individuals caged at the Buffalo Federal Detention Facility. Most of these individuals were held there on immigration related charges. During the COVID-19 pandemic, someone wrote from Thomas Feeley's jail "Being detained here, we are like the proverbial lamb waiting to be slaughtered."

LLOYD TACO, APOLOGISTS

Lloyd Taco is sorry it is eating Lloyd tacos on the way
to Buffalo Federal Detention Facility to feed
tacos to the brave prison workers who do not
feed people jailed indefinitely enough food for these people to
not lose weight indefinitely, some zero outside laughing
in the distance of someone else's third year w/o a lawyer—
so inside one works, if one can, hours for pennies to
pay the prison for just enough overpriced food-like commodities
to not get sick from a body eating itself from prison
provided starvation rations. Outside
jailers scarf pickled onions and queso-slathered nachos, inside,
if one can work or does not want to work for one's abusers,
one starves. Lloyd Tacos is sorry
it was sorry it was sorry it was sorry it was
feeding prison guards, all lives matter
to Lloyd Tacos as Lloyd Tacos eats gallons
of steaming beans and brisket,
truck doing donuts around Buffalo
Federal Detention Center, drawing zeros, crying out on
a bullhorn to someone who has not had tacos or burritos or nachos
or mangos or peaches or a Snickers bar in years—*feed me, feed me,*
feed me your prison dollars. Lloyd Tacos is sorry
that it was sorry that it was sorry
that it was sorry that is was sorry that is was sorry, please
says Lloyd's Tacos, free me from the starvation of shame, Lloyd Tacos
shall not die in this pit, Lloyd Taco's shall not fail—
Lloyd Tacos is driving to Buffalo Federal Detention Facility
to feed the work of starvation, Lloyd Taco
must drive to Buffalo Federal Detention Facility
to feed the work of starvation.
Lloyd Taco feeds the work of starvation.

COUPON: TO RECEIVE ONE FREE APOLOGY

W/ 16 OZ CUP OF REPTILE TEARS UPON
PURCHASE OF MEH TACOS PRINT AND
CUT OUT THIS COUPON
AND BRING TO LLOYD TACO

1503 HERTEL AVE, BUFFALO, NY

❶ Lloyd Taco's apology for feeding pigs appeared in several news outlets. Here's one: "Lloyd Taco Truck apologizes for serving lunch at Federal Detention Center in Batavia." After receiving pushback from, well, racists, Lloyd Taco cofounders walked back their apology four days later. The apology for the apology: "Chris and I want to fully and sincerely apologize for our past statement after our truck's visit to the Federal Detention Facility in Batavia [jail where individuals are often held indefinitely without charges or representation] last week. Out statement was hastily made, and we reacted too quickly to criticism we received for that visit." Not to be outdone, rival mediocre white-owned taco chain, Deep South Taco, hosted a fundraiser for white supremacist jail/slaughterhouse overseer Sheriff Tim Howard.

CHRIS JACOBS, MEMBER OF FAMILY THAT BUILT ITS FORTUNE ON CONCESSIONS MONOPOLIES[i]

Chris Jacobs takes the money he makes renting space
to ICE, folds it into a fat stack to strike
Chris Jacobs in the face, I'm just
a home town boy, he says, whacking himself
with money, Jobs, he says, whacking himself
with money, Holding cells, he says, whacking himself.
Eight dollar hotdogs, whack! Twelve dollar
Cokes. Whack! O yeah! he says, Let this wedge of static break my brain
dipped in gold, hung from my heart,
Whack! Whack! he says
running through the caverns
of a stadium in which he owns a concessions monopoly.
O yeah! I'm a hotdog! I'm meat!
I'm the only food
behind the one-way gate, Here I go, O boy,
jumping into the grinder—

i 250 Delaware Ave, Buffalo, NY 14202: The Delaware North building was constructed to house the Delaware North company. Sporting a modern façade, including a green wall, it also houses an upscale restaurant and hotel. Five floors above the clatter of silverware and people softening at a glistening bar is the Western New York ICE field offices, complete with a holding cell. And who is Chris Jacobs? No one really. A place, a creature where money, from circuits of extraction, and power, by way of that money, congeal.

BLIZZARD OF '22 KILLS 41. THE MAYOR BLAMES THE DEAD FOR THEIR DEATH.[i]

Mayor Byron Brown says do not leave home,
do not go outside during the blizzard while Byron
Brown wraps himself in another blanket in 14
Blaine where he just lost power in the howling pounding
howling blizzard don't go outside Byron
Brown tweets eating his last cold PB&J, fixings bought
with the last twenty of his last paycheck
washing dishes, the only job he could land with his kind
of record, don't leave your house Byron Brown whispers
in the frost-stenciled dark as snow pours through the window
frame empty now that the blizzard has ripped away the duct-taped
cardboard that served as a frame the landlord said
he'd fix the day he put down a 2,800 deposit and first-month's rent.
Don't go outside Byron Brown says to Byron Brown
as his phone dies the snow doesn't, his stomach groans,
his head separates from his head, looters are the
lowest of the low, Byron Brown says, pulling on his fifth
shirt, lowest of the low, as he just barely tugs on a pair
of slacks around his other two pairs of pants.
Don't go outside Byron Brown says
to Byron Brown as he picks up a hammer
descends the unlit stairs, hovers behind the icy door
lowest of the low, lowest of the low, he
whispers, time passes, lowest of the
low: you climb the stairs, you
open the door you're doubled over by hunger,

you get back under three blankets and a quilt,
you trudge through waist-high drifts,
you see your breath, you see your breath,
your feet are wet and the wind splinters needles
across your cheeks as you fall asleep and dreamless
dream trudging through your blankets
as if an anchor, as if a shroud, toward Buffalo's Golden
Corner where an incandescent bulb
burns over rows of chips, you turn in bed—on to what
side? It's so cold you're crowned in ice.
Lowest of the low, Byron Brown
says, don't go outside, as his heart
slows his elbow barely registers
numb-fisted hammer blows to the padlock
on the gates between Byron Brown and his life
Lowest of the low, Byron Brown says
to Byron Brown weeping in the cold, weeping into
his frostbite-bloated fingers. Don't go
outside, Byron Brown says to Byron Brown
in the cocoon of every fabric he owns
lowest of the low, coldest of the cold,
Byron Brown finds Byron Brown
ice-encrusted on the press-conference podium
at 14 Blaine Avenue, as he blames the dead for their death,
the pulse of his dream stops.

➊ On December 23, 2022, a 37-hour long blizzard began to pummel Buffalo. Residents were given little warning of the unprecedented intensity of the blizzard. It quickly crippled the city. On December 24th, the City of Buffalo issued the ominous tweet "No Emergency Services Available." During the blizzard and its aftermath 47 people died. Many of the dead were elderly. Many died of hypothermia inside or near their own homes on Buffalo's majority Black East Side. When Ruth Wilson Gilmore describes organized abandonment making people vulnerable, it is hard not to think of Buffalo's East Side, where municipal services have been withdrawn, reduced, and frayed for decades, softening it up for the devastation of the blizzard. The mayor's response was to blame the dead for their lack of preparedness and to vilify looters, many who were trying to survive in an environment where cold and unplowed, snow-choked roads and sidewalks limited their mobility to a radius of a few blocks for almost a week in which most stores remained closed.

MILLARD FILLMORE, FOUNDER OF THE UNIVERSITY AT BUFFALO

Niagara Falls: Millard Fillmore
drops a coin into the ramp of
the machine, the view unshutters
as he presses his eye to
the scope, trained on the crashing
ribbons, swarming mists—all the arcs
of shattering and reshattering
light—Millard swings the scope on
its turret, his view swimming across
the vertiginous, free-falling
emptiness of the gorge, a
border, wall, the inflection
point of so many laws his
heart smashed against with every
dawn severed from who he finds
at last peering into a scope
on the other bank, who shoots
a hand up, waves like a
hummingbird flies—his son
his son, that life—of course Border
Enforcement snatches him,
of course ICE abandons him
in a cage, lawyerless, and alone
with a memory of a view of
his son, waving across the Niagara.

/

Millard Fillmore exhumes Millard Fillmore's
corpse in the shadow of an obelisk
in section F of Forestlawn then
welds himself to his bones to a stanchion at the
center of the Niagara-spanning
Peace Bridge that reads *I Did*
Nothing—at the place freedoms
and unfreedoms meet and transform.
I Did Nothing.

❶ September 18, 1850, President Millard Fillmore signed into law the Fugitive Slave Act, which enacted strict provisions for returning runaway slaves to their owners.

MICHAEL PHILIPS, WESTERN NEW YORK ICE FIELD DIRECTOR, 2021 – PRESENTⓘ

Michael Philips points a gun at Michael Philips head
while Michael Philips sweats over the suds
Michael Philips' wife screams from the kitchen.
Michael Philips screams: "Hands up"
at Michael Philips over the cutting board,
one hand shoots up but the other won't stop
pointing a gun at Michael Philips' head.
Michael Philips' scream extends
until the dishwater goes flat.

& Michael Philips screams at Michael Philips screaming, trying to climb
each scream until Michael Philips' scream gives out
and Michael Philips can't speak at which point
Michael Philips' trial begins. Michael Philips' kid
is pulled from pre-K to serve as
Michael Philips' defense attorney. Consequently,
Michael Philips is deported to Michael Philips'
office on the 5th Floor of 250 Delaware Ave
where Michael Philips builds a wall on both sides
of the door—mission accomplished. In Michael Philips
office, Michael Philips points a gun at Michael Philips' head.
"Pure. Pure. Pure," Michael Philips says as Michael
point the gun at his head:
"Safe. Safe. Safe," Michael Philips says.

ⓘ **Say what's up to Michael Philips on LinkedIn.**

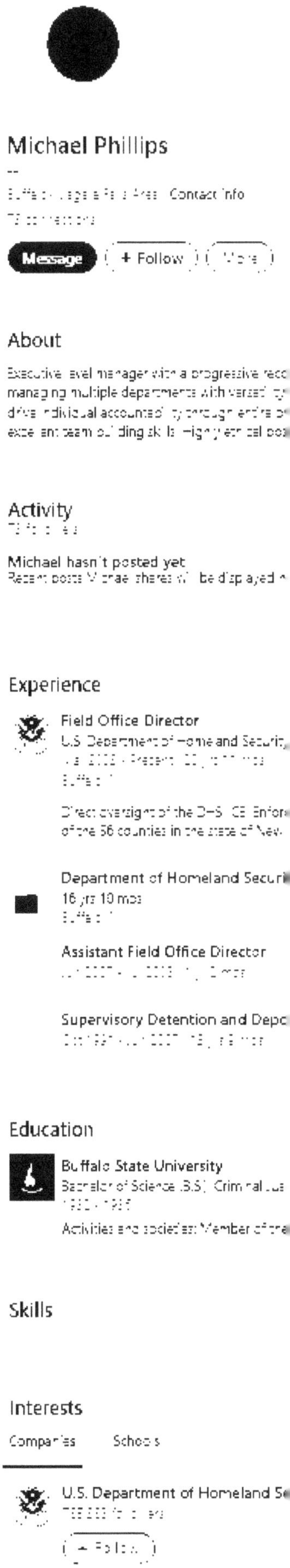

MICKEY KEARNS, ERIE COUNTY CLERK, WILL NOT BE GRANTING LICENSES TO UNDOCUMENTED IMMIGRANTS[i]

Mickey Kearns is in line at the DMW with his passport,
a passport that's gone thousands of rugged miles
through wannabe apartheid walls, past wannabe
apartheid cops, through the carnage of a
ten hour shift in the steamed kitchen in a strip-
mall called racial capitalism. Mickey Kearns is
in line at the DMV with his passport and signed
affidavit that says this is my life, my body, my being,
the vulnerability of being known to you,
the machinery of the state, so I, Mickey
Kearns can pick my sick and scared kid up from
school and hold them in their tenderness, so I, Mickey Kearns,
can, when the world is booming in the too
small studio of my skull, just take a drive, for the
hell of it and smoke and dissolve what's congealed
into anger into the freedom of motion this whole
land was conquered for—instead of shivering in
the Buffalo snow waiting for a bus that may not come
to take me to a job that's evaporating by the
second and a refrigerator emptying overnight

and a hope for myself growing further and further
away, so I, Mickey Kearns, am in line at the DMV.
I step up to the counter, I meet Mickey Kearns.
Mickey Kearns looks at Mickey Kearns. Says no.

❶ Mickey Kearns, local piece of shit, uses his position as the Erie County Clerk to fear monger, stating he would not issue licenses to undocumented immigrants, hanging signs at DMV customer service windows with ICE's tip line number, and filing a lawsuit in a federal court against a New York State law that provides access to licenses for undocumented individuals whose super-exploited labor New York's agricultural industry runs on.

LOUIS & PAUL CIMINELLI, DEVELOPERS[i]

Ciminelli buys Ciminelli from
                                        Ciminelli buys Ciminelli
from Ciminelli on credit what might be
                                        food flies into beds, trees,
porches, 30 year-old Kenmore
                                        cake-baking ovens fly from Ciminelli
into Ciminelli from Ciminelli
                                        to Ciminelli the big nothing 58.9
million into nothing Ciminelli
                                        asks for more millions to pour
into official looking emptiness
                                        Ciminelli must walk as Ciminelli
unhouses Ciminelli the void
                                        hungry to change the rules so
Ciminelli can inhale more of the
                                        homes bleeding from the piñata of
the city the void Ciminelli whacks on the day
                                        of his sentence/release into the artificial
extended downtown graveyard Ciminelli summoned for
                                        Ciminelli from a riverbend & broken stones
of a city-owned parking lot
                                        & repeat until Buffalo is a lonely
concrete dome Ciminelli gropes
                                        through bleeding his memories into the terrible
black hole that is his brother
                                        Ciminelli drags like a lead ball through every
empty street every empty house
                                        every empty book every locked door

printed w/this sutra for rent for rent.
the only for rent one you for
rent may know for rent is yourself
for rent Ciminelli for rent
for rent for rent

❶ Ciminelli, Jemal, Sinatra, Termini, Paladino—the developer class in Buffalo that jostle to line up at the trough for city subsidies—decades of our congealed labor—to throw up the kinds of buildings that say the city will never change and neither will the structure that guarantees who owns it, that guarantees that the median household income in some neighborhoods is less than 27k a year. Money, concrete, concrete dust—Buffalo stays poor. Sometimes the game gets so sloppy one of the players gets caught. In 2018, Louis Ciminelli was convicted for his role in a bid rigging scheme involving the state-subsidized Tesla GigaFactory. His sentence of 28 months was overturned by the U.S. Supreme Court shortly after it started. Ruling class solidarity.

GROVER CLEVELAND, FORMER SHERIFF OF ERIE COUNTY THEN MAYOR OF BUFFALO[i]

for Rob Galbraith

"I cannot rid myself of the idea that this City government, in its relation to the tax-payers, is a business establishment, and that it is put in our hands to be conducted on business principles."

—Mayor Grover Cleveland, AKA Big Steve

THE SCAFFOLD

Lake Erie steamers' wakes slap breakwalls cold wind rakes
plunges into the city
where Jack Gaffney, father of two,
Mary, Johnnie, shivers on the scaffold
before the jail where the library will be

Detective Jake Emrick drops a black sack
over Gaffney's head, between Gaffney
and the world canvas sheets unfurled
between the scaffold and thousands
come to see what it looks like: a killing

and here is a future president
hand on the iron lever,
eye on his watch.

GAFFNEY

Dead drunk 3 straight weeks—he
couldn't stop—Jack Gaffney
shot a man in the head
with the gun his brother-in-law handed him
after the man cleaned him out in cards
proceeded to rub it in
shot him in the head,
saw what he had done, washed
his bullet-broken face, sent for a doctor—
he couldn't stop—Jack Gaffney
shivers on the scaffold breathing
Buffalo's frigid air—breath—at last
through the black sack on his head
Steamers dock, loaded with skin and bone
scraped from the lakes, unpacked by uprooted
uprooting men Gaffney served
at his tavern in the First Ward.
Jack counts his life: one.

Grover Cleveland stands at the kill switch
to send a message to men like this
about who gets to do the killing.
Against the cold, waffled screen
of the executed's hood
Gaffney summons the faces
of—

RAPIST

December 15, 1873:
ten months after Sheriff Cleveland killed
Gaffney, he raped widow and mother Maria Halpin,
intercepted her on Swan Street,
invited her to dinner twice—insisted: Ocean Dining Hall
& Oyster House, 11 Swan, open just last year. Perhaps
roast mallard, French olives—insisted on escorting
Halpin to 39 Swan, rooms she shared
with her son. There, Big Steve--300lbs, 6 ft tall—
raped Maria Halpin. Grover Cleveland raped Maria Halpin.
Sheriff Cleveland raped Maria Halpin.
Future President Cleveland raped Maria Halpin.
The Sheriff told her, if she reported him, he'd ruin her
—even if it cost $10,000, even if he was hanged.
After Halpin gives birth
to a son, Oscar, Grover Cleveland, future
mayor of Buffalo, hires men to forcibly commit
Halpin to Providence Lunatic Asylum and
coerce her into giving up Oscar,
who they place in Buffalo Orphan Asylum.
Then Cleveland had Halpin smeared in the press.

HANGMAN HUNG

A west wind blows across the ice-eyed lakes, faster—
ruffling the gallows-encasing screen
Erie County Sheriff Grover Cleveland
looks at his watch: 2 minutes before noon.
He pulls the iron lever.
The lever releases the iron pin which holds the trap door.
Grover Cleveland is yanked five feet in the air.
For 23 minutes a chord closes even tighter
around his neck, the muscle of his throat and lungs
gasp against his whole weight. Grover Cleveland
pulls the lever on December 15, 1873. Grover
Cleveland is yanked by the neck from his bed on the corner
of Swan. Grover Cleveland pulls the lever
and in 2023 the earth erupts at 29 Greenview Avenue
Princeton, New Jersey and there Grover Cleveland's soil-
mottled skeleton hangs from a tree. Sheriff Cleveland
pulls the lever & Sheriff Tim Howard flies from his
rocker in Wales Township to the roof of the Erie County Holding Center
where he hangs thirty-two times for twenty-three minutes each
with a pillowcase over his head
and a spit mask bunched around his neck.
Cleveland pulls the iron lever and every year
nooses like snakes burst from the diseased tree
of his corpse—every time they cut him down
they hang him again and every Sheriff and President
and rapist and jail-cabled judge.

GOODBYE

The single job in this new dispensation:
each Sheriff executes the next
until there are none left to terrorize the world,
until there are none left to terrorize
those who stand up to the foreclosure
of their own good enough living
and the relations that make such life sweet.
Goodbye Grover Cleveland,
George Jackson is leading a procession of martyrs
out of the prison yards,
out of the shadows of sniper towers,
out of the digital reticule of drones.
Goodbye poem of endless retaliation
until tomorrow writes it again.

❶ Grover Cleveland served as the Sheriff of Erie County, in which Buffalo is located, from 1871-1873 then the Mayor of Buffalo from 1881-1882 before moving on to the governorship of New York State then the President of the United States. Mark Schneider: "Like his predecessor, Democratic President Grover Cleveland looked on silently as lynching soared throughout the South. William McKinley, the last Civil War veteran to serve in the White House, studiously avoided comment upon southern outrages like the Wilmington, North Carolina, massacre of 1898." While every American president is guilty of murder by decree, from Washington's organization of the genocidal Clinton-Sullivan campaign to Lincoln ordering the mass execution of 38 Dakota warriors to Obama's authorization of 542 drone strikes, Grover Cleveland is the only president known to have personally executed someone and committed rape. A golf course named after Grover Cleveland is located at 3781 Main Street in Amherst, a town adjacent to Buffalo named after a general who waged biological war against the Shawnee and Lenape nations via smallpox-inflected blankets.

THE RULING CLASS, THE PIG CLASS, EVERYONE, ALL

"Either poverty must use democracy to destroy the power of property, or property, in fear of poverty, will destroy democracy."
—Thomas Rainsborough, 1647, Leveller

Where do the ruling class organize?
Where should you organize?
What neighborhoods are the developer class trying
to crack, gas, & sterilize?

& if you were to pick a street, a block, a
home to hold with those the city has always tried to crush
as if it were a trench

where would it be?
Where does the mayor live?
Where do the cops organize?

in our weakness we dreamed a
spiral of guillotines a

spiral of guillotines.
Where are the jails?
Who makes red lines?

What's the pig class?
And when the pig class meets,

who's in attendance? hacking,
phlegm-lipped, salt-cheeked
glitching in the gap between

the velocity of the image
of a precinct burning and
Buffalo belly up

offering its organs
to carrion birds.
Who is left wounded?

What violence discourages organizing?
What salt-pitted street can you hardly escape?
Where will everyone see

whose violence law makes routine?
Does painting the powerful lashing
themselves further harm

those originally hurt? Satish Tripathi, President

of the University at Buffalo, must now work one job
on the Chipotle splatter line,
one delivering groceries
at 2 am, taking a stats final under twilight
sedation while a bottom-tier
prof gives plasma during a second
shift behind the wheel of the med school
mortuary van/dream-shredder in the exam

bubble *E: I hope*
in debt in debt-begotten hope friable
and glad to intern at the bank

that administers these debts which prove
I'm real in the pine-green bristles
of this carwash, I mean school as

organ extraction,
the one I need to fight
& love unto the madness I need.

388 Delaware Ave
The Buffalo Club

977 Delaware Ave
The Saturn Club

Burn it, take it, open it to flood.

Where do you take part in democratic processes in your day?
Do you take part in a democratic process in your day?
Verbs, not nouns, not babies, babies

kneel & kiss the toilet,
palmful of Erie water, great carrier

into the underworld, here are the ashes of a destroyer
C blessed.
Where would you sedate, exile, or re-educate the rich?

How do you feel reading descriptions of discipline?
Can we not see exploding militarism as an acceptably
mystified recommitment to a carceral state?
Who is talking up World War III

because they got sick of hearing abolition?
In a dream, the head of the Buffalo Water Board,
Oluwole McFoy's teeth fall out like a smashed piano's keys

since he silently pulled fluoride from the
city supply in 2015, it's not a dream McFoy
& Frédéric Van Heems, Pres & CEO of Veoli

who the city sold water service to in 2010, take
turns with a set of pliers, ripping each others'
incisors out, growing long gowns of lead and blood.

Unfired, McFoy wakes up in his office chair
with a toothache, its shaggy, bacterial root
growing upward into the furnace

of his brain.
Police have gunned down your neighbors.
Who did they kill? Where are these profane-

sacred sites? & if we consider killing
organized medical and/or psychological neglect?
& if you consider the whole pig class
down to the last real-estate agent/clown?

wounded w/counterinsurgency's tags
in what spaces does your language for love get lost?
Rocco Termini driving an excavator

across Brad Termini's lawn, launching
its shovel through the master
bedroom wall, swallowing Brad whole,

rending his dreams
in the snorting vortex of the shovel,

planting a tree in the crater of his son's
bed, propagation of local gentry

a thousand home-flattened lots
the city froze in amber.
Saint Abandon, Saint Extract,

Saint Apology.
Chamber of Commerce—Buffalo Niagara Partnership
257 W Genesee #600

unbroken by opportunistic weeds.
Post-police raid community outreach
just below this window where I peck

Mental Health officer in a halo guns,
new formation/routine.
Where in your city does whiteness express itself

as a militarized identity politics?
Where are the monuments of solidarity against that
—vertiginous portals

of hatred and love?
Where am I afraid to go?
& fuck whoever in the city

told the Debs guy he couldn't
plant trees in Peckham's vacant lots
because one day they might inconvenience

some developer's bulldozer's blade
like cops copy & paste the formulas the supreme
court provides, transforming crime into law.

The martyrdom of Saint Sidewalk smooth
enough for a wheelchair to roll.

The martyrdom of Saint Erie who once poured through
the mouth of the city sweet enough to drink
in a life getting longer

the martyrdom of Saint Sturgeon at the end of the
line cast into the Niagara

as it had been cast on another continent's shore, hook
sinking a hundred yards from a city sewage outflow.
Who could know the fever flushing Buffalo's drains?

Martyrdom of Saint Oxygen, Saint Breath
Well, you know how that story goes,

so imagine here a better and breathtaking poem
in which Buffalo's ruling class
makes a war of extinction on itself

under bright lights and flying cameras

cranes, glittering scaffolds.

They're wrapped so thickly in armor you
can't tell if they're dead,
they just don't get up,

a brilliant stillness
except the clanking of garbage trucks.
If everyone who organized

the poisoning and abandonment
of the most tender of us—
What land does your city claim? What will it do with it?

What water does your city claim? What will it do with it?
What oxygen does your city claim? What will it do with it?
All up and down, we pissed

on the mansions on Chapin Parkway
golden braid
that kept us together

no matter how long
no matter how far apart.
Officer Mark Andrzejak (salary: $137k) spinning piledrivers

Mark Andrzejak into the pavement
outside the marque of the Elmwood Regal
until he goes blind

& the pavement bleeds
2.9 million dollars
across a few lawns

from the Regal
his address falls out

14 Hartwell Rd, Buffalo.
Who will be organized into enough to bring forward
the Buffalo we need?

Will we be organized into enough to bring forward
the Buffalo we need?
to mark

each mark—ink, stone, cast-
iron etched metal, concrete—too still,
too silent to stand

for the strange revolutions
of a single sentient life—I mean
someone

just trying to do their thing
in the blocks that outlast us,

in the blocks that last with us,
where will we change with each other
so these blocks change with us?

❶ This one is too dense with grudges, wrongs, big systems and small things I've seen looking at my window and walking down the street to annotate it all. But we'll sweep up a few. In addition to having a Flint-dwarfing problem with lead in the water supply, the city silently stopped fluoridating the water in 2015. And as the city heads toward budgetary disaster it continues to pay out of pocket the costs of several lawsuits seeking compensation for police brutality, including a recent $43 million payout to a woman left paraplegic after a police cruiser ploughed into her. The city's budget is devoured by the police whose violence devours the budget. Money that could be spent preventing harm (lead remediation) is spent compensating for harm.

ALIENS—ABDUCTION

class is in session   flames find a grip

in   pigs clattering   in oily combs of skin.
Mark Polancarz (D) calling

the national guard   & squeeze, burn those grease pots

to ring hotels where the lifeboats flounder
spill in smoke—the pig class

interim undulated cop-faced plasm

flame horde sails of splintered   posters

dust blurred moon's ray
serrated mouth in Buffalo State President's

serrated mouth interim

undulated   cop-faced plasm   517
Cleveland Hall   evicted 44 &.   Oozes

—tardigrade-spliced exospheric
apparatus creature—from the mansion at

152 Lincoln Parkway   on 1.1

sterilized
city   acres   amaranthine star-chipped sky

dribbles into the black wine of   the lake
smoke I mean smoke—smoke settling

upon everything like the 'socialist' balling
a dirty sock into his mouth as soon

as the chittering suburban hordes burst

from their sulfurous burrows against

the precious vessel

(a strange ink poured over the world)

through firestorms, through a strange

ink poured on the world

my friend C picks up the phone: porcine-arachnid
death threat vocalization

put it on the pile   you can't know how my friends
slip between coordinates

the suburbs wrap the city

in a web of self-consuming flame
let gentle waves

lift these travelers through

so we may slip from the lights
that shave shadows from faces

to feed them into a vast and alien machine

let these lifeboats through

❶ In the summer of 2023, New York City bussed over 600 migrants to the Buffalo-adjacent town of Cheektowaga where they were housed in three hotels. The region spiraled into an anti-immigrant furor after two of the migrants were charged with sexual assault, resulting in the town of Cheektowaga hiring a law firm to help them find ways to legally displace the migrants, which they succeeded in doing. As a result of the xenophobic furor, Buffalo State University evicted 44 migrants from the dorms on short notice and the Democratic Erie County executive Mark Poloncarz demanded New York City stop sending migrants to Buffalo while also deploying the National Guard to hotels. Many of these migrants had been forcibly displaced several times already.

THE WAR AGAINST GAZA IS LOCAL

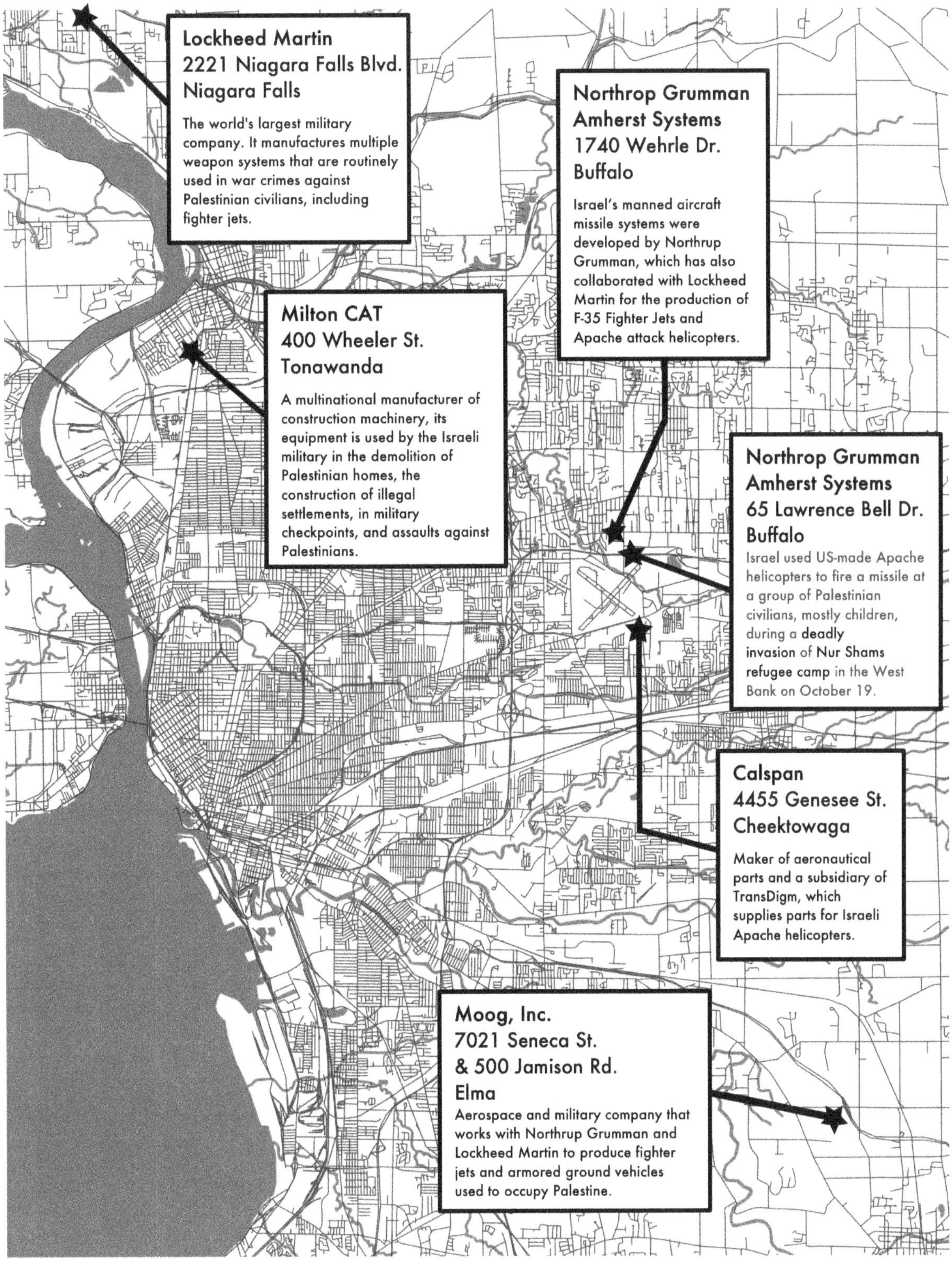

ACKNOWLEDGEMENTS

A version of this sequence first appeared in *Fugue & Strike* (2023) and is appearing again thanks to Black Ocean Press. A version of "Blizzard of '22..." appeared in the zine *some informal commons*, designed and printed by India Johnson. Seeds for several poems came directly and indirectly from the many, many reporters, record keepers, and community activists who kept these facts alive. Thanks to MC for comradeship in the production of agit-prop . Deep thanks to Mike Corrao for this killer design and whose enthusiasm for this project doubled it in size. Finally, this sequence owes much to the greater thinking, frameworks, or methodologies of Charisse Burden-Stelly, Ruth Wilson Gilmore, Gerald Horne, Ed Sanders, and Derek Seidman.

CLOAK

LEARN MORE AT HTTP://CLOAK.WTF

www.ingramcontent.com/pod-product-compliance
Lightning Source LLC
LaVergne TN
LVHW072124060526
838201LV00069B/4971

9798218391997